SURVIVAL FOOD TO STOCKPILE

The Ultimate Guide to Select, Preserve, and Stockpile Food for Self-Sufficient Living Off-the-Grid and Prepare your Pantry for the Worst of Catastrophes

Jonathan Henry

GET YOUR BONUSES NOW!

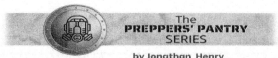

The **PREPPERS' PANTRY** SERIES
by Jonathan Henry

To walk you through the journey of learning how to build your pantry to deal with emergency situations, in collaboration with Bryan Burret, Margaret Ross, and Tammy Grant, I have created 3 guides for creating home healing remedies, using one's garden to get food, and foraging for food in nature that will help you get the most out of this book.

- Free Bonus #3 (eBook) -
MEDICAL HERBALISM
FOR BEGINNERS

- Free Bonus #1 (eBook) -
SELF-SUFFICIENT BACKYARD
FOR BEGINNERS

- Free Bonus #2 (eBook) -
FORAGING
FOR BEGINNERS

All these bonuses are **100% free**, with no strings attached. You don't need to enter any details except your name and email address.

To download your bonuses scan the QR code below or go to

https://jonathanhenry.me/free-bonus

Table of Contents

Introduction

What is a Food Stockpile?

A food stockpile is simply a collection of non-perishable foods, which can be stored in an area that is easily accessible during an emergency. This can be done by purchasing bulk items at your local grocery store or by making your own bulk foods from scratch.

Having a food stockpile allows you to buy the necessary supplies without having to worry about going into debt or having access to credit cards during an emergency situation. It also allows you to save money on expensive items like milk and eggs—which are necessary for many dishes—and makes it easier for your family members not normally involved in cooking or eating meals around the house (such as children) because they do not have access to those things at home either!

Life can be so unpredictable, and the world is always a little more dangerous than we think. Life is beautiful, but it's also terrifying. This can make us feel like we're not prepared for anything—and this is where having an emergency food stockpile comes in handy.

An emergency food stockpile is basically a stockpile of food that you have on hand to help you get through an emergency situation. It's not just about having enough food for a few days; it's about having enough food for weeks or months if you need it.

So how do you go about building an emergency food stockpile? It's really simple! First, figure out what type of foods you like to eat and which ones are easy to store at home. Then start collecting them in one place: your pantry, your freezer, or even just in Ziploc bags in the back of your fridge (if space allows).

You might wonder why some people think it's important to have an emergency food stockpile while others don't—but actually both groups are right! You can never predict what life will throw at us next—but knowing that we're prepared with a quick-and-easy source of nutrition could make all the difference when disaster strikes!

Why Should You Establish an Emergency Food Stockpile?

Emergency survival food stockpiling is very important, especially when you have a family to feed. You never know when disaster will strike and it's always better to be prepared than not.

When you are prepared, you can rest assured that your family will be taken care of in times of need. The key is having enough food to last them for several days without going into debt or going hungry.

The importance of having a food stockpile for emergencies is something that many people take for granted. We live in an age where the internet is always accessible, and we have access to foods from all over the world. It's easy to believe that if we have a few cans of beans and rice on hand, we'll be fine.

But what happens when you lose power? Or your car breaks down? Or your water runs out? What if there's no way to get food from outside your house because it's snowing? What if you can't buy any more gas because there are no stations open?

That's why it's so vital to keep some emergency supplies in place—just in case. And with this book, you'll learn everything you need to know about emergency survival food stockpiling so that when those situations arise, you're ready and able to handle them.

There are many reasons to have a food stockpile for emergency. The most important reason is that you never know when you might need one.

When we think about emergency survival food stockpiling, we tend to think about stockpiles of canned goods, but there are other ways to prepare. For example, if you have extra fruits and vegetables in your garden right now, save them! Don't throw them away when they're ripe—the same goes for any other produce that's ready-to-eat now.

Another idea is to make homemade stock or broths from the meat and bones from your freezer stash. You can use these recipes as a base and add whatever ingredients you have on hand (like spices or even wine). If you have some extra time on your hands, this is a great way to get creative with your stockpile!

If none of those are good options for you right now, don't worry! There are plenty more ways to build up your own emergency food stockpile.

In an emergency, it's essential to have a food stockpile in place. This book will help you learn how to build a food stockpile that will allow you to survive for as long as necessary.

Chapter 1:
Essential Foods To Have On Hand

The following is the list you should consider when starting your food supply. Remember it all starts with a plan so make sure you are recording your meals. This list is comprised of foods and items that quickly disappear once a disaster strikes. These are high demand foods and having a ready stockpile with these items dramatically increases your odds for survival should a disaster occur.

Water Is Still #1

You always need to make sure you have the proper amount of water available to you at all times. These items are very important but please do not overlook your water supply. Many preppers underestimate the amount of water they need to survive for an extended time frame. You should always remember that water is number one.

Your "Shelf-Stable" Supermarket Shopping List

Before we look at foods that are better to buy online or in bulk, let's look at an example of what a good supermarket "shelf-stable" shopping list would look like.

Be aware this list is just a guideline. Don't forget to consider the items that would work best with your family's needs and preferences.

Grains
Grains are essential ingredients to store in your pantry. They're calorie-dense, extremely versatile, and can store well.

- Oats
- Popcorn
- Flour (All-purpose and cake)
- Pasta
- Instant Mashed Potatoes
- Dried Corn
- Rice (White, long-grain, short-grain, or basmati)
- Cornmeal

- Quinoa
- Cereal (Most cereal has a shelf-life of 9 months, but when stored in an airtight container, it can last up to 2 years)

Beans/Legumes
Beans and legumes are superfoods for a reason! They're calorie and nutrient-dense and contain large amounts of fiber and protein. They're also easy to store and versatile to cook with like grains.

It's recommended to store dried beans/legumes that can be prepared using boiling water. You can also store some cans or cooked beans that can be consumed without any heat if you face an energy or water shortage.

- Black-eyed peas
- Lentils (Red, yellow, brown, green, or black – they're all excellent but black lentils are hailed to be the most nutritious type)
- Pinto beans
- Kidney beans
- Lima beans
- Chickpeas (Garbanzo beans)

Meats & Other Protein Sources
Meat is great for adding flavor to dishes and is a superb source of protein. Just be sure to consider if your group/family has any limitations with the meat they prefer or any limitations regarding religion or dietary choices. If you have a strict vegetarian in your midst, you don't need to starve the rest of your group of meat.

Ensure you have an adequate stockpile of typical meat alongside alternative proteins like tinned jackfruit, soy meat, or vegetable proteins. Don't forget to consider fish also!

- Canned tuna/salmon/mackerel/sardines
- Spam
- Canned Chicken
- Textured vegetable protein (TVP)
- Imitation Veg protein
- Jarred Vienna Sausages or Frankfurters
- Country ham
- Dry-cured ham or bacon

Many people tend to turn their noses up at canned meat; it's often labeled a "sub-par" variant of meat product. But you'd be surprised how much you can do with it! I wouldn't recommend consuming it straight out of the can, although it is safe to do so if you have to. Canned meat can be terrific when fried or sliced up and thrown into a soup or stew.

Dry-cured meats are a great thing to store, as a whole dry-cured ham will be good indefinitely (as long as it hasn't been cut into). Dry-cured food, unlike wet-cured food, doesn't require refrigeration.

Also, even if you're not a vegetarian, vegan, or pescatarian, don't shy away from eating products like textured vegetable protein. TVP will last up to 20 years if stored properly and can be a delicious meat substitute (as well as a fantastic source of protein).

Fats/Oils

Several fats/oils are essential for nutrition and the actual cooking process. Most types of fat will last between 1 and 2 years on the shelf, for both saturated and unsaturated ones.

- Vegetable Oil
- Olive Oil
- Lard
- Shortening
- Coconut Oil or Milk (good for curries)
- Peanut/Nut Butter (an excellent protein source!)

Most types of oils will only have a shelf life of from 12 to 18 months, so if you're looking for the best cooking oil to store long term, the best choice would be coconut oil - which can last up to 2 years if stored correctly.

Baking Ingredients

Things you use for baking may be labeled by many as "nonessential" items. However, many of these ingredients can be utilized in various ways (not just for baking cookies). However, you may find yourself in the mood for baking cookies on your homestead at some point, and if that happens, you'll precisely have the tools to do so! There's nothing wrong with a good batch of cookies sometimes.

- Baking soda
- Baking powder
- Cocoa powder

- Powdered milk (If you can't stomach powdered milk, it's good to have some small plant or soy milk cartoons in your pantry. They don't need to be refrigerated unless opened, and they have a shelf-life of around eight months – not too long but an excellent short-term alternative to fresh milk if you're looking for one.)
- Corn starch
- Yeast
- Vanilla extract
- Jell-o
- Instant custard mix
- Powdered sugar
- Syrup (Pancake syrup will be good for two or more years, while corn syrup will last forever. Be careful of syrups like maple syrup as it will need to be refrigerated after being opened.)

Herbs/Spices
Stockpiling plenty of dried herbs and spices is a great idea, as you'll find yourself slowly going crazy living off of food without them for an extended period. The taste and texture of boiled rice/oats without salt or flavoring are enough to drive anyone mad in everyday situations. Make sure to pack as many spices as possible in your inventory. Salt and vinegar have a ton of different uses and benefits, so these are ingredients that we recommend you stock in large quantities.

If you are storing these ingredients properly, particularly the salt, honey, and sugar, they'll last forever. However, after a few years, most spices/herbs will have a less potent flavor. Honey often has a habit of crystalizing after it's opened and stored for a long time, but this can be remedied by soaking the honey container in some warm water for a few minutes. Honey doesn't go bad. It just looks a little funny after a while.

Most of the spices/herbs are just suggestions. When considering what you want to store, think about the spices and herbs you and your family typically incorporate into your cooking. There's no point storing something like ginger if you have never used it and are not familiar with how to use it. This is a mantra that should apply to everything you store.

- Salt
- Honey (Good quality is better.)
- Granulated Sugar
- Vinegar (White, apple cider)
- Rice wine vinegar (Only necessary for cooking Asian-style rice.)
- Italian seasoning (These "combined" spices are great for convenience.)
- Cinnamon
- Soy sauce
- Chicken/beef/vegetable bouillon/stock cubes/granules
- Garlic powder
- Black pepper
- Chili powder
- Garam masala
- Cumin

- Paprika (Smoked or regular)
- Cayenne
- Ginger
- Coriander
- Nutritional yeast (Full of nutrients and has a savory, cheesy flavor. It's an excellent alternative for cheese in many dishes)

We've added these herbs/spices to this list as many supermarkets do sell them in large quantities, but these ingredients are often better bought in bulk from online or wholesale stores (such as Costco).

Food and Vegetables
Of course, most fruit and vegetables are perishable, so they shouldn't be included in this "shelf-stable" supermarket shopping list. However, there are some variants of fruit and veg we recommend purchasing.

- Canned fruit
- Canned vegetables
- Raisins
- Dried cranberries
- Dried sweet potato
- Dried banana chips

Considering the shelf-life of canned foods, fruit and vegetables high in acid will have a far shorter shelf life. This includes fruit and vegetables like tomatoes, grapes, blueberries, and pineapples. Canned tomatoes typically only last around 18 months but are extremely versatile, so growing your tomatoes is recommended. They can be canned to ensure a consistent supply of this ingredient (plus, tomatoes are one of the easiest things to grow!).

Drinks
When it comes to your stockpile, you have added water (and a little coffee), but have you considered any other types of liquid? Honestly, they're not essential, but having a packet of Kool-Aid or a few cans of Coca-Cola can be excellent morale boosters. This is especially important if you have kids on your homestead or caffeine addicts.

- Instant coffee mix
- Teabags
- Packs of Kool-Aid
- Powdered energy drinks (like Gatorade)

Food That's Better to Buy in Bulk

We just discussed what kind of food to look for when shopping in supermarkets, but there are several food types that you'll be better off purchasing either online or at a large wholesale store. This may be due to convenience, but it can also be a fantastic way to save money.

All the things in this list are perfect to buy in bulk as they all have a long shelf life.

Look at our list below to see what food we recommend buying in bulk.

19

- Pasta
- Rice
- Beans & lentils
- Salt
- Honey
- Oats
- Dried fruit
- Whole grains (such as quinoa)
- Whole popcorn
- Coconut oil
- Peanut/nut butter
- Vinegar
- Nutritional yeast
- Cereal
- Stock cubes/bouillon
- Plant milk

Let's look at a few items that it's better **not** to buy in bulk:

- Flour: Due to its short shelf-life, it's not ideal for bulking buying large quantities of flour
- Spices/herbs: Bulk buying spices and herbs is okay if they are stored correctly, but if you plan on keeping them for extended times, then the herbs/spices will lose their potency. If you'd like fresh herbs and spices around the year in a disaster situation, a great alternative is to set up an herb garden in your prepper garden and grow your own.

Chapter 2:
How To Start A Food Stockpile

Where To Start?

Food preppers should pay attention to some critical factors before beginning their stockpiling, and this is about shelf life.

When it comes to stockpiling food, shelf life is by far one of the most important factors that preppers must pay attention to. Although some foods have a restricted shelf-life, some foods exist that can be stored safely for the long haul, which can last up to many years.

The biggest advantage of having a food pantry is that it allows you to prepare for any unforeseen emergencies, be it short-term or long-term.

Numerous scenarios could happen and make it impossible to go to the store for essential food items. We have recently witnessed such a situation with the Covid-19 outbreak that led to panic buying and global shortages of many basic commodities, especially food. Other scenarios could also arise in the future, be it another pandemic, a hurricane, earthquake, tsunami, or even a biological attack.

Eventually, you come to realize that grocery stores do not store enough items for these kinds of situations. They usually only have enough food to provide for their community for roughly three days or even less. This means if an emergency arises, your local grocery store cannot cater to everyone's needs. So, is it not better to be safe than sorry?

This section will discuss ten ways to stockpile your food, where to start from, which foods to store, and how much to spend. The best way to go about it is to start simple and eventually increase it over time.

10 Ways To Stockpile Your Food
1. Think Through Your Goals

Before entering this phase, it is essential to think about why you want to do this. What are you trying to achieve? Are you focusing on the short term or the long term? Considering these points will allow you to organize your space accurately to your needs. This means you will gauge how much space you need depending on the duration of an emergency. You will know if you need extra containers or storage boxes to save any items, or will everything fit on your shelves? You will also need to consider whether you aim for a mini-market in your pantry to stock items in bulk or would instead use that space for something else like canned produce.

This is the importance of setting a goal; these are some generalized goals you could try to achieve with your food pantry storage. It is essential to define what role your food pantry will play.

a. Short Term

A short-term supply is about three months' worth of food on hand. The food can be a variety of canned, freeze-dried, or dehydrated ingredients for preparing meals from scratch. Keep in mind; that those nights of throwing a frozen pizza in the oven will be gone. Meal prep is going to take a little more effort. Think back to your grandma's time. She made everything right in her kitchen. She didn't have the option or luxury of a microwave to heat a frozen dinner. It is all about cooking the old-fashioned way.

It would be impossible to find a list of food you should store fit to be perfect for your family. Your family isn't going to eat the same food as your neighbor and their family. Nor will your family require the same amount of food as the couple down the road who don't have children.

Jot down what you would typically serve the family in meals for one week. If you wrote in McDonald's or stopped at 7-11 for breakfast, you need to substitute those meals with something from your kitchen.

Now take that list and identify and list out any ingredients you need to make every meal. Assume you will serve that meal once a week for the next 12 weeks. Multiply each ingredient by 12, and you have your list of items you need to build up to a short-term, 3-month food supply.

Let's go over some examples.

On Monday night, you serve the family canned chili with cornbread. You use two cans for the meal and one box of cornbread.

2x12=24 cans of chili for 3 months, assuming you eat chili for dinner once a week.

1x12=12 boxes of cornbread. Now, it is essential to point out that bread isn't going to be an option unless you have a means of cooking bread, i.e., a Dutch oven or solar oven. You can substitute crackers for bread if needed. If you are planning on making cornbread, you will need freeze-dried milk and eggs to complete the recipe.

That is just one example of a meal that can be prepared without electricity. As part of your prepping process, you will want to make sure and come up with ways of cooking and heating your meals.

b. Medium Term

It is time to start building up to six months of food. Using the chili example from above, you would need 48 cans of chili. That is only a single night out of the week. One meal out of the 21 you will need to provide. Are you getting an image of the amount of space you will need?

Before we discuss the food you need, we must discuss the space issue. A complete, long-term food pantry will require a great deal of space. You will need a full closet, pantry, or even a spare room to store all of your food. Shelving is a must. You don't want to put any food directly on the floor in case there is a flood, which can happen from a burst pipe or a busted water heater. The shelving should be sturdy enough to support a couple hundred cans of food.

You will also want a supply of food-grade buckets with lids on hand. These buckets are ideal for storing bulk items like grains, beans, and pasta. Adding Mylar bags to your buckets is even better. You can find these in bulk online. Place your beans, flour, or whatever you store inside the bags. Seal the bags and place their bags inside the bucket. This will extend the shelf life of your dried food up to 15 years or more.

The space you choose for your prepper pantry should be somewhat dark. You don't want any direct sunlight streaming into the room. This will age your food and cause it to become stale or spoil. The space should also be dry. Basements are often used for food storage. Install a box fan or basement fan to help keep the air circulating.

Your food pantry will also need to be temperature controlled. You don't want the area to drop below 50 degrees Fahrenheit or above 80 degrees. Another problem you want to avoid is pests. Pests can destroy a food pantry in a matter of days. You must monitor the area for intruders. Mice, ants, cockroaches, and anything else threatening your food supply must be taken care of immediately. You can typically see signs of an invasion. Set out traps, poison, or whatever is necessary to eliminate the problem at the first sign of trouble. Take steps to prevent further invasions.

c. Long Term

The golden number—one year of food on hand. This is something many preppers aspire to. It is a long road, but once you place that last can of green beans on the shelf, you will feel accomplished. You will have a sense that all will be okay no matter what comes your way. But your journey doesn't end here. You will want to keep adding to your food pantry. Why? There are a couple of different reasons.

- You can never have too much food on hand. If you have a lot, you will be sitting comfortably and will not have to worry as much when a late spring storm destroys your crops and limits the amount of food you can harvest. You will also have extra food that you can use to barter for other items you may not have. A healthy food supply also means you can share with those in need.
- If you are up to a year's worth of food, it has probably taken you at least that long to build up the supply. That means you have some stuff that is getting old. By rotating the old stuff out and replacing it with new, you will ensure your food is fresh when something does happen. A pantry full of expired or spoiled food is not going to do you a lot of good. You need to implement the first-in, first-out rule. Don't be afraid to add a new item to your pantry and pull out the oldest to serve for dinner.

The food you store in your pantry will depend on your family. You only store what your family eats today. Don't stock up on a bunch of canned spinach or sardines if your family doesn't eat them.

They are not suddenly going to have a change of heart. Of course, if they are genuinely starving, they may choke it down, but they will not be happy about it.

It is just as important you diversify your food supply as well. You don't want to focus all of your energy on stocking 300 cans of chili. Your tummy will not be happy. You and your family members can indeed suffer from a condition known as food fatigue. Food fatigue happens when you eat the same food day in and day out for an extended period.

The condition causes intestinal upset, vomiting, diarrhea, and stomach cramps. You cannot afford to get sick and possibly dehydrated when medical attention may not be readily available.

2. Size of Family

Family size is a factor to consider because it will determine the quantity of food you need to store and the type of food you have to stock.

If your household comprises kids, you must stock up on easy, less time-consuming, and nutritious items.

Foods like nut or seed butter, mac and cheese, pasta, and pasta sauce are some items you should have on your list. You can add olive oil, spices, maple syrup, apple sauce syrup, and cheese to make food combinations. These items are great pantry staples for kids with a stable shelf life.

However, if your household consists of teenagers, the items you should stock must be in large quantities.

Food items such as white rice, microwaveable snacks, canned meats, lentils, and soups must be on this list for older kids.

When making a list of items, add a few luxury items to the list because if there's an emergency, you can guarantee that there will be stress; such food items can help reduce family stress.

3. Budget

Establishing a budget beforehand will keep you from going overboard and help categorize your items based on priority. This will ensure you do not purchase unnecessary items or too many of the same foods.

Remember that the budget is for food items and storage and shelving of those items.

This could mean purchasing storage containers, wooden shelves, custom-made ones, or even building them yourself to save money.

A realistic budget should be put in place to ensure you and your family's needs are met during an emergency.

4. Location

Another factor to consider is where you plan to store your items. This is probably the most crucial factor as it will determine the life of your food items.

The food storage location should always be a cool, dry place that is out of sight. If you have a basement, it is usually the best place to store such items. However, not all homes have a basement, which is not a problem.

Any cool, dark closet will do. If you live in a small apartment with little space around, it would be best to use spaces like the top of your closet or under your bed, for starters.

5. How Much Food Will You Stockpile?

Before deciding on how big your stockpile needs to be, you have to look at your family size like we discussed above, but we also have to look at your living location. Is it easy to access convenience stores, or are you living in a secluded area? These factors should be thought about before diving into stockpiling food.

6. A Food List

It will take you some time to develop a stockpile food list. You will have to review your inventory and note what you don't have and what you might need.

7. Take Time To Build Your Supply

This process is not done overnight. It will take weeks or even months to build a food storage supply. It is recommended to start slow and develop your pile over time, slowly and gradually.

8. Spend Time On Finding The Right Deals

This will be time-consuming, and you have to search for sales and the best deals available. You should regularly check online flyers and cashback apps for regular discounts.

9. Refrain From Buying Too Much

Beginning a stockpile process can become addictive, and you may get carried away. If you find good bargains, don't overbuy items because they are cheap. Go according to your list and the budget you have planned.

10. Be Aware of the Prices

Keeping up with individual products' costs will help you when you have everything on your list for half the price. This is so you can shop from cheaper areas every few weeks rather than every couple of days.

Cooking Without Power

Cooking can become a challenge after a natural disaster. Let's look at other cooking methods you can use if you don't have electricity but still want to cook a meal.

Charcoal or Gas Grills

This is the easiest cooking method when there's no heat or power. These should not be used indoors.

These indoors can increase your risk of dying from carbon monoxide poisoning and your chance of setting off a fire that could cause severe damage to your home.

Camp Stoves

Camp stoves can be used with gasoline or other solid fuel similar to the grills.

An electrical generator can be used to power small appliances that you use to cook your food.

Fireplaces and Wood Stoves

Wood can be used to cook meals in many cases. If your chimney was not damaged during the disaster, you could still use a fireplace for cooking. You shouldn't light a fire there if your fireplace has a damaged chimney. Make sure the damper is not closed. You should also ensure that the stovepipe is intact if you plan to use a wooden stove for cooking.

Eating Uncooked

However, this does not mean you have to eat everything raw. This applies mainly to fruits, vegetables, and nuts. It can be refreshing to have a light meal instead of a heavy, warm meal in the summer.

Bobcat Cooking Stove

This stove is excellent for emergencies and is very useful. The stove uses ThemaFuel cans, which allow it to be used indoors. It doesn't emit toxic fumes. One can provide a steady flame for approximately four hours and be reused multiple times. A simple way to look at this is that one can cook up to six meals. This can be used as an emergency backup or as a portable stove on outdoor adventures.

Solar Grill

This is a newer option and can be pretty expensive. It is an excellent option because it allows you to cook with power and sun. This can be used outdoors or as a substitute for an outdoor grill. This is an excellent alternative to traditional cooking methods. It is unsuitable for all climates, so it may not be worth the investment.

Disposable or Instant Grill

This stove is an affordable alternative to an emergency stove that you can keep in your stock. This allows you to prepare a warm meal using a biodegradable option.

Jet or Rocket Stoves

Another option is this. These stoves can quickly boil water and produce an intense flame. Rocket stoves use wood, while jet stoves can burn gas.

Outdoor Cooking

There are some things you should keep in mind when you decide to cook outside and build a fire:

- You should not build your fire in a carport.
- Fires must be contained.
- You can place stones or a drum of metal around the fire pit.
- A charcoal grill is a great place to make a wood fire.

- You should never use gasoline to light a fire, whether you're using wood or charcoal.
- After you're done, make sure to extinguish any flames.

Let's now look at some ideas for food since we have learned how to cook food without power. Food without power does not mean canned or packaged food that lacks flavor or taste. Consider these delicious meals you can make even if there's no power.

Meal Ideas for When the Power is Out
Instead of viewing a power cut as a disaster, see it as an opportunity to be creative with what you have. You can find many recipes that don't require any cooking. It wasn't so long ago that food could be prepared without power. With a bit of practice, we can do it again.

Breakfast

You should eat yogurt first if you have it. It will spoil after four hours without power in the fridge. Mixing yogurt with granola, muesli, or fruit can enhance its flavor. This makes a delicious breakfast or a snack for midday.

Oatmeal can be found in many disaster food pantries as a nutritious staple. Combine the right amount of oatmeal with water. Even cold water works. Allow it to rest covered for at least 24 hours. Then, in the morning, you can add any toppings you like to enhance its flavor. Fresh fruit like bananas, apples, and cinnamon are great toppings. If you require more protein, you can add nut butter.

You can also choose a cereal with shelf-stable dairy. Many bowls of cereal are high in nutrients and low in sugar. While shelf-stable milk substitutes and milk can be stored for a long time, they must be kept refrigerated once opened. You can also keep powdered milk in your pantry and use it to mix with water.

You can also make bread with butter or jam. This bread is not the healthiest option on this list, but it's a good choice for those who want a quick and easy breakfast.

Entrees

Salads can be a simple, easy way to make a meal. You will need to use fresh fruits and vegetables to create the recipe. Mix everything and chop it up. This will likely not provide enough food so that you can pair it with bread, canned corn, or cooked grains. You can make simple dressings from oil, vinegar, salt, and/or lime juice.

A good taco filling can be made with primarily canned ingredients. Chop tomatoes, beans, and corn. You can also add fresh avocado and cilantro if you have them. Combine all ingredients with lime juice, honey mustard, salt, and pepper. You can also eat the taco shells as a salad or with chips or bread if you don't own any.

A simple tuna salad mixed with beans is another great way to get more protein into your diet. White kidney beans, garbanzo, and cannellini beans are all great options. Mix the various options with some tuna drained. You can add onion, lemon juice, and olive oil to your liking. You can mix different kinds of beans to make a unique and delicious salad if you don't have any tuna.

You can save any kind of lettuce from going to waste. You can give your salad a unique twist by adding chicken or tuna. You can make a simple filling from a can of chicken, tuna, or salmon. Add celery, onion, and salt to taste. To make sandwiches or wraps, you can use tortillas or bread. You will feel fuller for longer if you add extra carbohydrates.

Rice paper spring rolls are a fancier option. These are quick and easy to make, despite what you might think. Any vegetable can be used, but the best choices are green or purple cabbage, bell peppers, lettuce, cilantro, and beets. Follow the instructions on the rice-paper container to assemble the vegetables. You can make a peanut sauce if you have fresh ginger, peanut butter, almond butter, maple or brown sugar, and soy sauce.

A burrito bowl is another creative option. To make this dish, you can use fresh vegetables and canned foods from your food supply.

Pre-cooked grains are still necessary for this recipe.

Chopped tomatoes, canned black beans and chopped avocado are all great options. Your availability of fresh ingredients will determine the dressing you use. Don't use any dairy products if the power is out for more than four hours.

Vegetable noodles can be made more accessible with a spiralizer or peeler. You can use yellow squash, carrots, and zucchini as the best vegetables. Drizzle olive oil or hard cheeses over the top if you have any. You will need to cook them differently if you don't like raw vegetables. This is the best choice.

Snacks

Even if you don't have power, there are simple snacks that you can make.

Peanut butter or another nut butter is a good option. You can also pair it with fresh bananas and apples if you have them. This snack is healthy and sweet if you don't have sweets or chocolate.

You can also make hummus to accompany your chips. Mix a can of chickpeas with lemon juice, salt, pepper, and any other spices you prefer.

Peanut butter and jelly sandwich is another classic option. This is comfort food that can be very helpful in stressful situations.

Chapter 3:
How To Organize and Manage Your Food Pantry Efficiently

How to Organize your Pantry?

When the disaster is about to strike, and you have just a couple of days left to respond, you might not get access to any of the resources or stocks in the supermarkets and local stores. It is because the last-moment preppers will rush to the markets and get their goods on a first-come-first-serve basis. And this is when the latecomers will not get sufficient stocks to withstand the entire duration of calamity and its after-effects. Therefore, you need to act early and have the proper sense of responsibility for organizing the supplies.

Irrespective of whether you have a small or large set of supplies, it is essential for you to organize all of them effectively to access necessary items at the time of need. For instance, if someone is experiencing a massive allergic reaction, you need to have immediate access to the anti-allergic medications in hand to save that person's life. Imagine not finding the box of medicines in your storage area! Things could be catastrophic! Similarly, if you have a baby amidst the calamity, they will need a variety of food. And you must be accessible to all of them throughout the survival period to ensure the healthy survival of your baby.

Store just the Foods you Eat

One of the avoidable mistakes the preppers make is stocking up on everything that catches their attention. The amateur preppers think about gathering food, regardless of whether they want to eat it. They pick up every other item that they see in the supermarket! If that seems edible and shelf-able for the long term, they prefer to buy and stock it. But this is a very wrong approach! You should only stockpile food and beverages you would like to consume, even at the worst times.

Wasting money on unwanted foods will start a different financial crisis within your family. There might be an urge in your mind to stock up your fridge and storage pantry with food supplies throughout the year to be able to tackle all kinds of unpredictable threats. But, you should be smart about what you intend to buy!

Make Use of Heavy-Duty Shelving

Apart from stocking up on food, you should also invest in making necessary arrangements for decent shelving. If you intend to keep your food in a heightened space and keep it away from any kind of water leakage and pests, count on getting heavy-duty shelves, which will help you maximize the storage space. You can go for metal shelves or some durable plastic shelves, as they are preferable choices with the necessary strength and ease of cleaning over time.

Moreover, these shelves should have the potential to handle the weight imposed upon them. The canned goods and food buckets are pretty heavy when you buy them for a survival stockpile. The worst organizing mistake is to pile all the supplies on the floor without setting them up properly. As a result, it creates a tremendous mess in the storage room that makes the goods inaccessible at times of emergency.

Apart from that, if you are using low-quality or weaker shelves to store your food at height, they would eventually fall apart and cause a lot of wastage. You need to check the manufacturer's details or the material strength upon withstanding the weight of supplies before finalizing your shelving material.

Maintain a Spreadsheet

If your emergency food system is running over a rotation system, you need to stay on the top of the sheet. It means that you should prepare a list or spreadsheet of what emergency items you have, what you have used from it, and what you have to stock back. This is the on-system organization of the survival food supplies within the prepper's pantry. You do not need to use a pen & paper to prepare your spreadsheet. Instead, you can use your Excel Spreadsheet over the laptop and keep track of it. If you intend to have a hard copy of the same, get a printout if you think you might not have access to the laptop at any crisis.

This organizational approach might not be the most brilliant idea. Still, it is one of the most significant ways of ensuring that the emergency food supply is available in good numbers and readily usable at all times.

Most rookie preppers prefer to consume the supplies from the survival stocks within the pantry that are about to expire. Following that, they forget to stock those things back! As a result, when the calamity strikes, they go low on food, which might risk your life and your family members. The foods you use as the rotation of your supplies should be marked in the list and highlighted for a refill or restock.

Additional Tips for Organizing the Food Pantry

Apart from these evident considerations, there are a few other essential tips for seamless and organized food storage for your pantry:

- **Group the Similar Items-** If you intend to adapt the ease of finding the items even more conveniently during a crisis, you should count on keeping the similar items nearby or together. For instance, you should keep the canned vegetables and beans together, the dried mixes on the second shelf, etc.

- **Count on Labelling Everything-** Without labels, it might be challenging to identify the boxes with different items. It might frustrate you at a time of need. You will eventually panic when you cannot just recognize the boxes in an emergency. Therefore, label everything, whether a small or a big box and do not hesitate to add a tag over it for its contents.

- **Add up More Shelves-** If you have some corner around the storage room or pantry that is not used more often, you can prefer to add more shelves to those corners. This will add more storage space around the room for you to stock up on even more supplies.

- **Have Some Tote bags-** Tote bags are easy to handle, carry or grab in case you need bugging out fast. Suppose your vehicle is not that spacious to carry many tote bags. In that case, you can install a rooftop carrier over your vehicle to be prepared for emergency transportation of goods along with you. Do not pack the heavy food items over the carriers, as it might overload the vehicle. You can use the carrier for sleeping bags, clothing, and other light essentials. Hence, this will free up the space in your vehicle for more food and drink supplies within the tote bags.

Hence, this is the ideal way to seek a proper food pantry organization. If you follow all of these measures, you will eventually be able to free up a lot of space within your storage sections. Use those leftover spaces to pile up other survival essentials within the same room but a little farther away from the food supplies. If there is any spillage, it might just cause damage and wastage of survival essentials. So, keep this factor in mind if you share the food storage room for other essentials.

Finding Room for Food Storage

Finding space for food and water storage is one of the most challenging aspects of emergency food storage. You will have enough space at the right temperature if you have a large house, garage, basement or cellar.

But not everyone can afford this luxury. People can live in mobile homes, condos, or apartments. These people don't have much space to store food or water.

There are many innovative ways to store three days' worth of emergency food or water if you fall into this category. Let's take a look at some of the options.

It's not impossible. It will take some creativity to find enough space to prepare food and water in case of an emergency.

- **Stairwell Space**

You've likely experienced the mess under your stairs if you have stairs. This area can be used to create shelves or place buckets of food along its back wall. Then, you can add a board over it for other food items.

- **Above the Washer and Dryer**

Because of its high heat and humidity, the area above the washer/dryer may not be ideal for many people. This area may be suitable for some canned goods or Mylar bags of dry goods like rice, beans or oatmeal if you rotate your food regularly.

- **Closet Storage**

Closets can often be more profound than necessary to store hanging clothes. Sometimes, you can add a shelf to store canned goods. You can use the extra space, but it won't compromise your clothing.

The shelf above your clothes is another space that could be used in your closet. This area is often used to store junk. You can clean out the space and use it to store emergency food supplies.

- **Behind the Door**

An inexpensive shoe organizer that fits over the door is another shelf option. This can be an easy way to store canned goods and bottled water if you have a small amount of emergency food or water.

- **Behind the Sofa**

You can push your couch against a wall and use the space to store food or water.

- **Under the Sink**

If food is sealed well, it should not be stored in this area. A large shelf can provide small to medium-sized side food storage areas to store soda or juice jugs containing rice and beans.

- **Extra Cupboard Space**

This is an area that many people overlook, but it is self-evident. This is often the dead space at the back of top cupboard shelves. You can do the same thing as with your closet shelf and clean out your pantry before storing your emergency food supply on these shelves.

- **Above the Refrigerator**

Sometimes, the refrigerator's top is too high to reach and can be too deep to store items we use frequently. You can store emergency food supplies in the back of your refrigerator.

- **Bookshelf Space**

You might consider removing books from the shelves and storing canned food behind them if you have a collection of books.

- **Under the Bed**

This is an excellent option for people who don't have a lot of space. You can also use bricks to raise your best. You can then slide a bin underneath the bed to store all of your emergency food. A twin-sized bed can often hold a three-day food supply for two people.

You can also consider other furniture if the space below your bed isn't needed. There is usually room underneath a chair, sofa or other furniture. You can store many items here. You can store food items here and move other items into these areas to make space for emergency food and water storage.

- **Utilize Empty Suitcases**

Most people only use their luggage one to two times a year. Your empty suitcases can be used to store food in bags or pre-packaged goods. You might consider putting all your food in one large bag. If you have to evacuate, you can pull out the bigger bag and fill your suitcase with the needed clothing. You can also grab your suitcase, and all your food is ready to go.

- **Buckets in the Bathtub**

Although this isn't the best situation, it can be cumbersome and may not suit everyone. However, this should be considered if you don't have any other options.

You might consider some food buckets that are well filled and sealed.

These can be placed in the bathtub and covered with a shower curtain. You will simply need to get the buckets out every time you take a shower.

Ensure your bathroom is not too hot, which could spoil your food storage.

- **Loft Storage in the Garage**

You can build loft storage if you have a garage but little space. This is great for high ceilings. You can also put shelving on the garage's upper perimeter. This space can be used to store emergency food and water. You can also use it to store other items in your home to make more room for food or water.

Mistakes To Avoid When Storing Food For Emergency

It can be challenging to come up with a practical food storage plan. Whether focusing mainly on commercially packed freeze-dried foods, store-bought canned items, or food preserved at home with a pressure canner, everyone seems to have their preference and opinion.

But each offers its benefits and drawbacks regarding price, portability, convenience, and package space.

Whatever your opinion on food storage is, there is one thing that all preparedness enthusiasts share.

We all want our food stocks to still be fresh, edible and nourishing for as long as possible. The last thing we want is to find ourselves in a position where the food items we store are spoilt.

And it takes ongoing effort to overcome the six challenges of food storage: temperature, oxygen, moisture, light, pest, and time. But with experience, we all learn to manage them as best.

But what about some of the other elements that could hinder food storage? Let's take a look at significant mistakes people frequently make while trying to put a long-term food storage plan in place:

1. Storing Food That You Don't Like:

Storing food you loathe or won't eat is a common mistake many make when storing food for emergencies. Think about it: We've all bought something when it was on promo sale because it was such a great offer.

But if it's something you don't like, what gives you the impression that you will eat it later?

It is foolish to spend money and use valuable storage space on food you won't eat just because they are sold at a bargain price.

If you're in an emergency, you'll probably eat anything. However, we're talking about preparations you make in advance rather than a last-minute scramble when the pantry is empty.

2. Not Taking Note Of Out-Of-Date Foods:

To avoid this mistake, put a label on all your food items indicating their date of purchase. You can keep a log, a notebook, or set reminders. Additionally, you can choose to clean your pantry once a year.

Rotate your food supplies in storage as much as you can. While manufacturers place "use by" and "best by" dates on canned and packaged foods, many dates are more about taste and texture than actual spoilage.

3. Keeping Everything Together In One Place:

It is not suitable to store all your food items in one place, as anything that happens to one can affect all.

Mason jars containing home canned products need to be fastened to their shelf with a bracket or cordage.

Canned goods should be stored on a shelf off the ground.

You wouldn't want to happen to have your food jars tumble off the shelf to the ground and break during an earthquake, storm, or any other disruptive event.

Always consider the potential for disaster in your place of residence when planning your storage locations.

4. You Lack The Cooking Skills:

Do not buy a food item you cannot cook. It makes.

If you don't use them, you have no sense in having them stocked in your pantry.

But you can learn to prepare these foods early enough to have a library of recipes at the ready should the need arise.

5. Storing Up Staple Foods, While Leaving Out Comfort Foods:

While you eat well and maintain a balanced diet, you should also make room for occasional indulgences. Kettle Chips are a real indulgence, especially the difficult-to-find non-salt variety.

6. High Or Unsteady Storage Temperature Conditions:

High temperature is one of the destroyers of food storage. It significantly affects the shelf-life of any food, especially when storing it up for the long term.

Also, temperature fluctuations can be just as damaging to your food items as high temperatures. While there might be no scientific data to back up this claim, from my personal experience, I have discovered that food stored at a steady 80 degrees will last longer than food stored at 25 degrees in the winter and 87 degrees in the summer.

7. Not Storing Liquids To Rehydrate Dried Goods:

While there will always be a place in your pantry for freeze-dried foods, the liquid in canned fruits and vegetables affords you an additional source of hydration. Also, freeze-dried foods can be rehydrated using the drained liquid.

8. Failing To Provide Other Sources Of Fuel For Cooking:

You'll need a fire source or portable stove for your cooking if electricity should go out. Propane stoves and rocket stoves are very affordable and are good alternatives.

Also, remember that you will need fuel for your stoves, whether from sources you collect (like biomass) or buy.

9. Lack Of Variety In Storage:

You will need various dietary items to get an entire balanced nutritional content from your meals. Even more so, most people require variations in their meals. This is particularly important for kids still developing, the elderly, and people with disabilities who may already be selective eaters.

10. Keeping Food In Improper Or Cumbersome Packages:

Although you might differ, it's much easier to package food in manageable portions. This becomes even more practical if you have a small family. And if you're storing up for short-term emergencies, you can easily pull out what you need without repacking the entire storage.

Store various food items in the same bucket is another recommended practice. Have a bucket with different foods and the appropriate condiments, rather than one with only one sort of food. So, instead of stressing out and searching through a dozen or more buckets to find what you need for meal preparation, you can have one bucket that contains everything you need in enough proportions.

Also, avoid storing your food items in a container that has been previously used. For instance, do not store your beans in a bucket that was once used to keep pickles without first putting the beans in a Mylar bag. In the same vein, ensure your food storage containers are moisture and pest-proof and that they have not previously been used to store-up toxic substances.

11. Buying A Food Kit Without First Checking Its Content:

Before making a purchase, check out the content of the food kit and gauge how many of the included items you'll need. Also, consider the cost of the package, and decide whether it will still represent good value for your money if you don't need all the content.

12. Relying Solely On Food Reserves For All Of Your Meals:

No matter how large your food store is, it is wise to consider other food sources. You can add fresh vegetables from your garden to your food supply with enough light and space. You can also grow some herbs that have medicinal value in addition to being healthy food sources.

In addition to gardening, explore the potential local bounty that could be obtained via foraging, fishing, and hunting. A local abundance of some kind can be found in most places, including berries, fish, deer, and even the common dandelion. Learn all the necessary skills required to transform them safely into edible foods.

Importance of Food Rotation

To put it another way, the pantry in your home is a living, breathing organism that needs to be cared for by being fed and hydrated regularly.

It is designed to be used routinely, except in an emergency. Since you are stockpiling the foods that are a consistent part of your family's diet, it won't be difficult for you to maintain the freshness of the food and use it up before its expiration date. Always remember the guideline that states "first in, first out," which stands for "first in, first out."

Set up a process. You may keep the older items in the centre of the shelf while moving the more recent meals to the rear. You may also store things from left to right, taking things from the left and putting new things from the right.

It is an alternate method. You may arrange your canned goods in a manner that is practically foolproof by using shelving designed for food rotation. It ensures that you are aware of what you need to consume first at all times. A portion of the things I keep in long-term storage is on a "ready rack" in my kitchen. If you're anything like me, you like doing a little "shopping" in your kitchen by moving from your large pantry to your more compact one.

It allows you to review your stockpile and determine which products need replenishment. Examine the label to determine when the product should be discarded. When deciding on the product's quality or freshness, you shouldn't base your decision on the purchase date.

If the bulk products or other things do not have a date stamped on them from the manufacturer, you should affix a label with the date you purchased them. It is important to mark and date all home-canned and preserved goods with the date they were processed and stored for storage. When you review your inventory list regularly, note any items not being used up as quickly as you had anticipated.

If you and your family do not like using a product, do not put off getting rid of it until the day that it is set to expire. If you don't want to toss it out, you may donate it to the local food bank instead of throwing it away.

It is important to do frequent rotations of the grain and other bulk materials stored. Keeping more goods on top of the ones you currently have in storage is not a good idea. First, the fresh product should be placed in the container, and then the older product should be poured. Take your time, and don't rush through this procedure. The excess should either be stored for subsequent use or dumped into a separate container designated for later use.

Food Storage Equipment, Tips & Kits

Two of the most significant factors responsible for the rotting or degradation of stored foods are moisture and oxygen. Microbial development can be facilitated by moisture in dry foods. Moisture in the vicinity of metal canned foods can cause rust and eventually undermine the can.

The presence of oxygen influences many foods' quality decline. Packaging that prevents moisture and oxygen transmission is required to keep goods for an extended time. Acceptable storage containers include bags, glass canning jars, plastic PETE bottles, and plastic buckets.

Mylar Bags

Mylar bags are made of multilayer laminated plastic and aluminum. Because the food is separated from aluminum by a food-grade plastic layer, there is little risk of contamination.

These bags protect food from moisture and insects, but they allow for a small amount of oxygen to enter and are not rodent-proof. If you want to use Mylar, placing those bags into a bucket is usually a good idea to protect them from rodent damage.

Typically, these bags can last up to 5 years, or 20 if you add oxygen absorbers and vacuum seal them. Each gallon of food should use one 300 cc oxygen absorber or 2,000 cc oxygen absorbers per 5-gallon bucket.

Make sure that when you use Mylar bags, you use a heat-sealing device to seal them entirely. If you want to vacuum seal them and secure them using a traditional vacuum sealing device you already have, you can do that too.

This requires a bit of creativity, but if you know what you're doing, you can make it work well.

Mylar bags are typically smooth, while vacuum-sealing bags have textured sides to create channels for the vacuum sealer to suck the air through.

By taking a few snips out of your bags, you'll be able to create those channels on your Mylar bag as well. Put two small snips, maybe 1 inch by 2 inches long, on each corner of the

Mylar bag, with maybe a ½ inch sticking out the top. Place it into your vacuum sealer, and allow it to suck out all the air. This will take longer than you'd typically expect vacuum sealing to work since there will only be two small channels to use, but it should suck out all the air.

At that point, you can use the heat seal setting. Do this twice; your bag should be secure and ready to go.

Mylar bags should be kept in some other container to prevent them from coming into direct contact with cement or walls. Remember that these bags don't stack well, so they can be a bit of a mess to store well. Your best bet is to store them in large 5-gallon bags and place these in large square buckets.

Keep in mind that foods with over 10% moisture content risk developing botulism in a low-oxygen environment, so make sure that you only pack dried goods, such as rice, beans, pasta, oats, flour, and sugar. Freeze-dried foods will also do well, but you want to avoid foods rich in oil or moisture.

Cans

If you need to store low-oil content, dry, and shelf-stable foods, cans are a great option. However, you must ensure an enamel coating between the food and the metal to keep it food-safe. Cans are traditionally kept in most stockpiles. However, ensure that you have a manual can opener if you choose to stock up in this manner.

Like Mylar bags, it's recommended to use low-moisture foods to prevent reaction with the metal. While many liquid foods may come in cans, they are unsuitable for longer-term storage. Dry foods should be stored with oxygen absorbers, except for sugar.

Unlike Mylar bags, however, these can prevent all oxygen from entering the cans. They can rust on the outside, so you want to keep them somewhere without moisture. They should not be kept in direct contact with concrete. Typically, you can use a rolling rack to store your cans. Just make sure you label them so you can tell what's in each can.

A #10 can holds 3 quarts and is suitable for 2.8 pounds of rolled oats, 3 pounds of macaroni, or 5.5 pounds of pinto beans. It may also store other foods, and you can open them in much smaller amounts than if they were stored in large buckets.

Polyethylene Terephthalate (PET) Bottles

Polyethylene terephthalate (PET) bottles can be good options if running low on other types of storage. However, you should only use PET bottles if you're storing dry goods, as they don't provide much moisture barrier.

To identify which bottles you have PET, look for "1" in the recycle symbol. It may also say "PETE" or "PET" underneath the symbol. These bottles should have a screw-on lid, which should also have a plastic or rubber seal. For example, 2-liter soda bottles are made in this manner. You can reuse these; ensure they're cleaned and dried well. If you've ever used the bottle for non-food purposes, don't reuse it.

You can store rice, corn, beans, and wheat in these bottles for the long term or use them short term for other foods. If you are storing long-term, use one oxygen absorber packet per bottle. Keep in mind that these options must be protected from light and rodents. These options aren't as efficient as Mylar or canning, but they are still effective in a pinch.

Plastic Buckets

Large plastic buckets are another great option, but you must ensure they are food-grade. They must also be free from other food items. If you've used them for non-food items in the past, don't use them. You can either store food in its original packaging for added protection, or you can choose to use the bucket itself to store things with liners.

Buckets are typically the recommended options for storing food long-term in larger quantities, but keep in mind that oxygen can enter them. It's a good idea to use Mylar bags to line them. Then, ensure you store them off the floor without stacking more than three buckets on top of each other to protect the seals.

Grains, flour, sugar, and other dried foods store well in these containers. They are also among the least expensive options for sealing. Remember that you should only choose food with gaskets in the lid seals.

Glass Jars

If you want to store smaller quantities of something, using glass jars is one of the most effective ways. Their smaller sizes make them convenient and can be reused several times, so long as you don't accidentally drop and break them. They are air and watertight, making them quite efficient, and rodents can't chew through them without significant difficulty and injury. However, because glass is transparent, you need to keep it protected from light to prolong the life of your food.

Factors That Disrupt Long-Term Food Storage

These five factors water down your effort for long-term food storage. Therefore, you should try to ensure that these factors are absent in your food storage location to avoid the degradation of your foods. These factors include:

a. Oxygen

As surprising as it may sound, oxygen is one of the factors that downgrade your long-term food storage efforts. Oxygen is not suitable for your food production because it triggers an oxidization process. Once the food is subjected to oxidization, the food can quickly go rancid/bad and lose its flavor. Also, oxygen encourages breeding microorganisms like bugs and bacteria because these microorganisms thrive in an oxygen-filled environment. The best way to handle the situation is to use oxygen absorbers to suck oxygen from food containers. The microorganisms will have no other choice than to leave the food container or stay there and die.

b. Temperature

The temperature around your food pantry matters a lot. The ideal temperature should be from 40 degrees Fahrenheit to 70 degrees

Fahrenheit. A warmer or hotter temperature can cause your food to lose color and vital nutrients (especially foods that contain vitamins A). The temperature should be stable because a rapid fluctuation of temperature in the room also causes a loss in food quality. For instance, a rapid change from 40 degrees today to 70 degrees tomorrow and back to 40 degrees the day after tomorrow can decrease the quality of the food. Always note that your food loses half of its shelf life for every 18 degrees increase in temperature.

c. Moisture

Moisture always comes in the form of condensation and humidity. Dampness or moisture on food, especially dry food, will likely turn the food into a breeding place for bacteria and moths. Besides that, moisture also breaks down the materials used for packaging, which can lead to food degradation. 15% is the ideal humidity level. Stay in a location with a high level of humidity. You can use better packaging materials like plastic containers with lids, jars, and canning or seal bags to regulate the food's humidity.

d. Light

When you bring your food in direct contact with natural light, the energy in the light will be transferred into the food. This will cause degradation in the food's taste, appearance and nutritional value. The natural light mentioned here is sunlight. Foods properties that are mostly affected by sunlight are fat-soluble vitamins such as Vitamin A, D, E, and K and proteins.

e. Pests

Dirt and moisture can attract pests into your food pantry. Pets include rats, mice, cockroaches, and moths. You can use oxygen absorbers to create an inhabitable environment in your pantry.

Stocking up on Pet Supplies

When you have brought a pet to your family, it is your responsibility to take care of them, irrespective of the challenges and situations you encounter. Every pet owner needs an emergency survival kit, especially for their pet. There are many human food pantry stocking options, but pets need a specific diet to stay healthy and fit. Just like you are vulnerable to the after-effects of any crisis, pets depend on you for help. They will rely upon you to feel safe amidst disasters or crisis periods. Therefore, just like you have stored your prepper pantry for the human members of the house, it is essential to have a separate shelf to stock up the pet supplies.

It is quite impossible to teach your pet to do the needful stocking and storing of food for the calamities that are unpredictable and might intervene in their peaceful lives anytime. You cannot expect them to take care of themselves amidst the crisis. The fur babies need your guidance and support, just like your kids. Therefore, have a separate pantry with your favorite pet food, treats, drinks, medicinal solutions, and other essentials. Remember that if you are bugging out, you must carry a sleeping bag and many other essentials for your pet, apart from just food. But at this point, we are mainly discussing bugging in the house with a food pantry. So, in that case, you should focus primarily on stocking food, water, and medicines for your pet for at least a couple of weeks.

The things that you should add to your pet pantry are:

- Bottled water is sufficient for a couple of weeks for each pet.
- Food for around one or two weeks for each pet. The pet food should be stored in water-tight containers.
- Water bowls and pet food.
- Manual can opener
- A list of essential medications with specific instructions
- Flea, tick, and heartworm medications for a whole month.
- Other medications for at least the next 2 weeks.

You should carry these basic things for their comfort and ease of survival amidst the crisis. Pets are more fragile than humans and might experience massive distress if they miss their usual routines. Therefore, stockpile your pet's sufficient food, drink, and medication items.

There are different needs of essentials that you must carry if you are bugging out with your pet. Apart from food, water, and medications, you might also carry a set of toys that your pet loves to play with. It keeps them occupied and diverts their minds from stressful situations while sheltering outside. Bugging out should always be the last option when you have pets, kids, and a big family! But if the situation forces you to leave your house for safety, you should take some necessary measures.

How To Store Pet Food and Treats

Pet food plus treats should be stored properly to preserve their nutritional content and to have information ready in case of a problem. Proper storage also keeps your pet from consuming too much of his food or getting into the cat's strict diet.

Follow these safety recommendations for keeping pet food plus treats to help maintain your pet healthy:

1. Pet food plus treats should be kept within the original jar or bag. In the event of malfunction or recall, you'll be able to quickly access the UPC, brand and manufacturer, lot number & "best by" date.
2. If you wish to keep dry pet food within another container, dump the entire bag inside the container instead of pouring the kibble straight into it.
3. If you want to transfer your dry pet food to another container, ensure it's clean, dry, and has a secure cover. A cover helps keep the food fresh while preventing your pet from eating it.
4. To remove remaining fat and crumbs from the storage container's surfaces, wash and dry it between completing one bag of the kibble and then filling it using another.

5. Dry pet food plus unopened canned food should be kept in an excellent, dry location. The temperature must not go beyond 80 degrees Fahrenheit. The nutrients may be broken down if exposed to too much heat or moisture. If the pet is particularly persistent or cunning in getting into his pet food, keep it in a safe place.

6. Refrigerate or discard unwanted or leftover canned or pouched pet food as soon as possible. Keep your refrigerator set around 40 degrees Fahrenheit.

7. After each usage, wash and dry bowls of pet food and scoop utensils, water bowls should be cleaned regularly.

8. Keep pet treats inside a secure area to prevent your pet from consuming the entire supply at once.

9. Like many other foods, pet food plus treats could be contaminated with hazardous germs that cause foodborne diseases. Following the above safe handling practices may reduce your chance of contracting a foodborne disease from tainted pet food.

Chapter 4:
Different Methods of Food Preservation

You can use several inexpensive methods to preserve fresh foods by canning, drying, or freezing them. Once you understand the basic procedures, you can use them to ensure you have nutritious food for your family in emergencies.

Canning

The first preservation method to consider is canning. Canning involves putting food into sanitized jars and vacuum sealing it to keep out contaminants and bacteria. While commercially canned foods can be a helpful staple, they also contain preservatives, chemicals, and large amounts of salt. If you preserve foods, you can guarantee that the food you are storing is free of chemicals and unhealthy ingredients. There are two similar techniques you can use to can your food.

Water-Bath Canning
Water bath canning or hot water canning is a process of canning that uses boiling water in a large kettle. Simply put, it involves placing filled jars into the water and boiling them until the jars have reached an internal temperature of 212° Fahrenheit for a specific duration of time. Water bath canning is excellent for fruit juices, jellies, jams, fruits, fruit spreads, salsa, tomatoes with added acid, sauces, pickles and condiments.

Here is a step-by-step guide to water bath canning:

1. Read through your recipe and instructions, and prepare the ingredients and equipment. Follow the guideline for the jar size, recipe preparation, and processing time.
2. Quality check – Check jars, lids, and bands to ensure they are safe. Jars with irregular rims, cracks, nicks or sharp edges may prevent sealing or be liable to break. The underside of the lids should not be uneven or have an incomplete sealing compound, as this may result in improperly sealed jars. Make sure that the band fits your jar perfectly.
3. Clean jars, lids, and bands in hot soapy water rinse well, and dry.
4. Place the jars in hot (not boiling) water until ready to use them. Fill a large saucepan or a stockpot halfway with water. Ensure the jars are fully submerged, leaving them full of hot water. You may also use dishwashers to clean

and heat jars. Keep the jars hot when adding the hot food; this will prevent the jars from breaking. Leave the bands and lids a room temperature for easy handling.

5. Prepare tested preserving recipes using fresh produce and other quality ingredients

6. Remove your jars from the hot water using a jar lifter; empty the water inside. Fill each jar with prepared food, and don't forget to leave headspace.

7. Remove any air bubbles in the food. You can use either a bubble remover, a headspace tool, or a rubber spatula. Slide it between the jar and the food to release the trapped air. Repeat 2 – 3 times.

8. Wipe the outside of your jars with a damp cloth to remove any food residue. You can now proceed with applying the bands and seal them tightly.

9. Place the filled jars in the canner until the canner is full. Lower rack with jars into the water, making sure to submerge each jar entirely in the water. Put the lid on the canner, then bring the water to a full rolling boil.

10. Process the jars in the boiling water for the time indicated on your recipe. You can turn the heat off when the process is finished and remove the canner lid. Let your jars stand in the canner for around 5 – 6 minutes to get them acclimated to the outside temperature.

11. Remove the jars from the canner, then set them upright on a towel to prevent the jar from breaking due to the sudden temperature change. Leave the jars undisturbed for 24 hours.

12. Lastly, check the seals on the lids. The lids should not flex up or down when you press the center. Once you have tested them, you can remove the bands and try lifting off the lids with your fingertips. If the seal is good, you will not be able to lift the lid. You can still refrigerate or reprocess the product if the lid does not seal properly.
13. Clean the lids and mason jars.
14. Label your preserves. Ensure to include the date so you can use food before it expires. Store it in a cool, dark, and dry spot for up to a year.

Pressure Canning

You will need a large kettle that produces steam in a locked compartment to use this canning method. You will need to heat your filled jars to an internal temperature of 240° under a particular pressure measured by a dial on the canner cover. Pressure canning is ideal for processing vegetables and low-acid foods such as meat, poultry and fish.

Here are step-by-step instructions for pressure canning.

1. Ready the pressure canner as needed, including jars, lids, ring bands, and other helpful accessories.
2. Wash your jars, lids and bands in hot soapy water, rinse well and dry.
3. Heat the jar in hot water until it's ready for use. Follow the instructions listed above under water bath canning.
4. Fill the clean hot jars one at a time. If necessary, you can consider reheating the jars by immersing the jar in the canning kettle full of hot water.

5. Remember to leave at least an inch of headspace to allow for expansion of the food.

6. Remove any air bubbles that have formed. You can use a bubble remover, a headspace tool, or a rubber spatula. Use the same method you would use for water bath canning.

7. By using a clean damp cloth, carefully wipe the jar rim. Any food residue around the rim may prevent the jar from sealing properly.

8. Remove lids from the hot water and carefully place them on the jars. Plunge the lids into cold water. If the lids stick together, then dip them again in boiling water. Screw the ring bands on as tightly as you comfortably can.

9. Place a rack in the canner, then fill it halfway with hot (not boiling) water.

10. Place jars on a rack so the steam can flow around them freely. Do not pack the jars too tightly.

11. Securely fasten the canner lid.

12. Heat the canner to the highest setting until the steam flows from the vent port or petcock.

13. Keep the heat high for at least ten minutes as steam flows, and then close the petcock. It will pressurize for the next 3 to 5 minutes.

14. Start timing the process and watch the dial gauge until it shows that the interior has reached the recommended pressure.

15. The weighted gauges should rock about two to three times per minute. Presto canners should rock slowly during the entire process.

16. Turn the heat off. Remove the canner from heat to let the canner depressurize.
17. Never force-cool canners. Force-cooling will result in food spoilage or loss of liquid from the jars.
18. Once the canner has depressurized, open the petcock. Wait about 2 minutes, unfasten the lid, and carefully remove it. Keep the lid away from your face to avoid getting burned.
19. Remove the jars from the canner, then set them upright on a towel to prevent the jars from breaking. Leave the jars undisturbed for 24 hours.
20. Lastly, check the lids to ensure they are tightly sealed and do not flex up or down when you press the center. Once you have checked the seals, you can remove the bands and test the lids to ensure you cannot easily remove them. Remember, even if the lid has not been sealed correctly, you can refrigerate or reprocess the product.
21. Put on a label, making sure to include the date. Store your preserved food in a cool, dark, and dry place for up to a year.

Drying

Drying food is one of the oldest methods of preserving food. People have been drying food for centuries, a simple, inexpensive way of keeping food edible for a long time. As with canning, there are several different methods you can use.

Sun Drying
The oldest and most inexpensive way to dry food is by using the heat from the sun. This method works best for fruits because they have a high amount of acid and sugar. This method is not optimal for drying meats and vegetables.

Ideal conditions for sun drying your food include a temperature of about 85° F. Drying foods on a day with a constant light breeze is preferable since the airflow will help lift moisture from the fruit. Very humid weather is not a good time to attempt drying food as humid air has a high moisture content that may lengthen the drying time. The humidity of 60% or less lends itself to this form of drying. If you live in a place where it tends to be very humid, you may want to stick to using a dehydrator or your oven. If you decide to try sun drying food, use this method:

1. Prepare the equipment needed in the sun-drying process. You'll need a rack or screen. Placing food on a rack will ensure adequate airflow around the food. Placing the racks or screens on top of concrete surfaces or aluminum sheets will help by increasing the temperature. The higher the temperature is, the more rapidly the food will dry.
2. Make sure to use food-grade quality materials for the racks or screens. Screens made of Teflon–coated fiberglass, stainless steel or plastic are ideal for sun drying. Avoid racks or screens made of copper, hardware cloth or aluminum, which are hazardous to human health.

3. Protect the drying fruits from insects and birds. You can use another screen or cheesecloth to prevent pests from your food.
4. Leave the fruit under the sun until it is scorched. Because heat, weather and humidity can slow the process down, you must keep an eye on the fruit. Once it is entirely dry, store the fruit in an airtight container.

Food Dehydrators
A food dehydrator is your best option for preserving foods with a low acid content, such as meats and vegetables. The convenient thing about using a dehydrator is that it takes away much of the guesswork. You can just follow the manufacturer's instructions for drying food. As with sun-dried foods, store the dried meats and vegetables in airtight containers and make sure to date them so you can rotate out food before it goes bad.

Conventional Oven
If you don't own a food dehydrator, you can also dehydrate foods in your oven if they hold a consistent temperature under 200 degrees. The ideal temperature is 140 degrees. Slice, trim and blanch the food first. Then put it in a single layer onto a baking sheet. Place it into the oven with the door open several inches to allow moisture to escape. Drying times vary for different foods, so do your research.

With any dried foods, make sure to watch them for several days after you have dried them. If you notice some moisture accumulating on the inside of the storage container, the food is not completely dry. Doing this properly may require a little experimentation, but it's an excellent method to ensure your family will have adequate food.

Freezing

The purpose of freezing is to delay all kinds of spoilage. It keeps the food safe with the growth prevention of microorganisms and slows down enzyme activity. The water within the food will freeze and take the face of ice crystals. Hence, the food becomes completely unavailable for the microorganisms that need it for growth.

Most of the microorganisms will stay alive even when the foods are frozen. Therefore, they need to be handled through different cooking means before freezing or defrosting. The nutrient content of the food doesn't get much affected upon freezing preservation. Some vegetables or fruits are blanched right before freezing to inactivate the yeasts and enzymes to avoid spoilage, even within the freezer. The blanching process is accountable for deteriorating some of the Vitamin C content in the food. Even with these losses, there are still high in overall nutrients.

The fruits or vegetables should be frozen immediately in the peak condition after being harvested. If this is approached, the nutrient contents will be preserved and reliable as survival food within your prepper pantry. There is no loss of vitamins or minerals for poultry and meats upon freezing preservation.

Protein contents are also unaffected due to the freezing methods. But, when you defrost the meat and poultry foods, fluid is lost. This liquid consists of water-soluble vitamins and several mineral salts. Therefore, you need to recover this liquid to ensure that these nutrients persist while cooking the meat or poultry.

Why Choose a Chest Freezer?

Chest freezers are the best equipment for freezing foods and preserving their nutrients. One should choose a chest freezer for its energy-efficient performance and ability to preserve the food for longer. You can also use the upright freezers, which demand low maintenance and are organized easily. They also have auto-defrost options, various storage accessories, and accessible configurations.

But even with all of the benefits of the upright freezers, the chest freezers are still the preferable option for the preppers. It is because the chest freezer preferably sits lower to the ground and has the capacity of storing more prepping food than other models or variants of similar types. Moreover, such freezers also have an upright door for you to store or access their contents easily.

What to prioritize when the freezer space is limited?

No families would count on buying multiple chest freezers to accommodate all possible emergency foods. Therefore, it becomes crucial for people to prioritize the essentials over the top rather than just stuffing anything they see first. Here is the list of items that you should count on storing first if your freezer space is limited:

- Meat
- Fish
- Whole chicken
- Roasts
- Soups
- Fruits
- Vegetables
- Milk, etc.

These are the priority things you should store in an ample amount for your survival necessity. These food items would help you sustain a better life amidst the crisis, as they are rich in enormous nutrients. After storing all these frozen items first, if you still have some space, you can put in all the frozen meals you bought for prepping. If there is some space, then storing cookie dough can also be an option for having a snacking source within the survival pantry.

Tips on Freezing the Food for Prepper's Pantry

Irrespective of whether you are using a chest freezer or an upright freezer, there are a few implementable things that you should prioritize the most. To help you with the impactful knowledge, here are those things framed in the form of tips on freezing for you to relate:

- You need to cool the foods before you go ahead and freeze them. If you are freezing the food when it is hot, it will work upon increasing the temperature of your freezer and might defrost other foods within the chamber.

- You should refreeze the goods only if you intend to cook any of them in between. For instance, you should only defrost chicken if you are about to use some portion of it and then refreeze it for further storage. Frequent defrosting and thawing processes will eventually promote the growth of bacteria over some food items, which will eradicate the nutrient contents.

- It is better to have a full freezer to run seamlessly and economically. It is because the cold air is not in desperate need of circulating too much. Therefore, minimal power is needed for the purpose. If you have a lot of space around your freezer, you prefer to fill it with half-filled water bottles. They will act as the gap fillers. Hence, it will contribute to your savings on energy bills.

- When storing your foods for freezing them in the chamber, you need to ensure that they are appropriately wrapped. You can wrap or put them in a sealed container before storing them in the freezer. Without this measure, your food might experience freezer burn and lose its nutrient potential & taste.

- In an emergency or when a calamity strikes, there might be a chance of a power outage for a specific period. If that is the case, do not open the freezer immediately to access those foods. Prefer to use the other options within your prepper pantry and let the frozen foods stay at a cold temperature within the chamber. If you have food in the freezer, you might need to get to the bottom of your power outage problem.

Freezing the food is one decisive way of preserving your favorite meals and items for the long term. Any time you feel like you are running on some crisis and there is about to be a shortage of food supply for your home situation or as a country threat, you will have the most nutritious foods ready in your freezer for access. So, while prepping your pantry for emergencies, count on getting a chest freezer over time.

Pickling

Pickling is an ancient method that the grandparents used for a long time to preserve food items. Technically, it is preserving edible food products with some acid solution. People generally use vinegar for this purpose.

The Benefits of the Pickling Method

To help you understand how pickling was/is one of the ideal preservation methods, here are a few of its benefits that have been statistically and practically proven:

- Pickling the food prevents the item from spoilage in a short period. It increases the shelf-life of an edible item.
- It reduces the overall food storage and preservation costs. You don't need expensive equipment to increase the shelf-life of your food.

- Pickling doesn't just preserve the food but also adds proficient flavor to it; therefore, for a long time, people are also using this method with the perspective of flavoring the existing dishes or using it in several other culinary applications.
- Fermented and pickled foods are excellent sources of nutrients such as amino acids, vitamins, and healthy bacteria.

Pickling Methods

There are four methods of prickling: quick pickling, salt-brined pickling, fermented pickling, and vinegar-brined pickling.

- **Quick Pickling-** The items that undergo pickling through this method are trimmed, chopped, sliced, or left as a whole. In some specific cases, these items are also blanched before they can be pickled. The item is packed in the canning jars, and hot pickling liquid is poured into it. The liquid is usually a mixture of water and vinegar.
- **Salt-Brined Method-** Here, a salt-brine process is executed where the water content of vegetables is drawn out. This helps the pickling liquid penetrate cells thoroughly, adding flavors to those items. The vegetables are doused with salt for a couple of hours before they are pickled.
- **Vinegar-Brined Method-** This process repeats the same procedure of drawing out water from vegetables. But the steps involve soaking, draining, and again soaking the

food item in a vinegar solution. It is done to offer a savory texture and flavor to the vegetables.

- **Fermented Method-** This method uses salt-water brine, and all vegetables are covered. The vegetables are weighed down into the solution and are left to ferment at an ideal temperature. The salt will help eradicate the vegetable liquid, and the microbes will occur naturally. The food develops aroma and delicious flavors.

Fermentation

Fermentation is a living process. Fermented food is an excellent means of preserving food; it adds a lot of flavors and is also excellent for good gut health. A little bit of kimchi or sauerkraut in the morning can be a great way to keep your gut working in peak condition.

If you can 'can' something, you can pickle something. Fermenting something is an old way of preserving it, and it is as easy as adding salt, vinegar, and time.

Food disintegrates and decays when left alone. Fermenting is the process of controlling that natural process. Microbes such as mold and yeast eat the sugars and starches and leave behind gasses and alcohol. The object of our controlled fermentation is to allow the bacteria and microbes we want to do their job and keep out the bad ones.

There are three ways to ferment: lactic, alcoholic, and acetic.

For veggies, we use lactic fermentation, which creates lactic acid that gives the food a distinct, tangy flavor. This needs to be done in an anaerobic, meaning oxygen-free environment. Therefore, the things we ferment need to be completely submerged in liquid.

You can use the same kind of jars for fermenting that you would use for canning, and you ought to clean them just the same. Wash the vegetables, too. Chop any vegetables to your preferred size so long as they can fit in the jar. Then add water until they are completely covered. I mean entirely; a tiny bit, even 1/16th of an inch exposed above the water, can ruin the whole jar.

Then you add salt. The amount of salt you add is a simple equation. The salt's weight equals the combined weight of the vegetables and water, multiplied by 0.025. For example, if the veggies weigh 6 oz, and the water weighs 3 oz, you need 0.225 oz of salt. $(6+3)*0.025 = 0.225$

Lid it and then shake it until the salt is completely dissolved. Remember, the veggies must be completely submerged at all times, so once the salt is dissolved, it's okay to open the jar and move the contents around or push them down. Some people will add an object to help push or weigh the food down, which is a perfect solution if they are being pesky.

If the cap is placed on tightly, the gasses will stay in and become mildly carbonated. Some people prefer that. If you don't, you can leave the lid on loosely or use a small airlock to allow the gas to escape. Some people barely leave on a lid, just enough to cover it, so dust and insects don't get in. That's not a problem.

Try to keep your fermenting veggies at about 60–75 degrees F. If you can't find a good place in your home, you can dig a deep hole in the earth and bury them there to keep them cool and out of direct sunlight. This was the traditional method in Korea for making Kimchi, and many families in the country still do it that way. Just be sure to leave a marker, so you don't forget where it's buried.

Within a day, the good microbes will eat off all the bacteria we don't want in our fermentation process. Lactobacillus will start eating sugars and converting them to acids. You might start seeing bubbles in four to five days, which means it's doing what it should. The longer it goes, the tangier and funkier the flavor will get.

If you don't submerge them well, you'll find mold growing on the exposed bits, and you'll know it's ruined.

Vacuum Sealing

Air is the primary carrier of oxygen, moisture, and contaminants that spoils food. The basic concept of this method is that if we successfully prevent the air from reaching the food, we can reduce early spoilage risks. For this reason, vacuum sealing is used for all types of food items, whether perishable or non-perishable; in both cases, the shelf life of the food is extended. This method can be applied to food items stored in mylar or aluminum bags. The vacuum is artificially created inside the bag by removing all the air.

First, take a clean and food-grade aluminum pouch or mylar bag, then place the food inside the bag. Now hold the sealable edges of the bag in your hands and submerge the rest of the bag in a bucket full of water; the air leaves the bag as it is lighter, and the water outside the bag exerts pressure.

Once the air is removed, seal the bag immediately and store it in the refrigerator, freezer, or any other suitable place.

Dry Ice Process

The dry ice technique also works on a similar concept; in this method, the effort is made to remove oxygen from the food. Whether you are storing food in a bag, PETE bottle, or food bucket, you can easily use this method and ensure the minimum growth of microbes and insects inside the food.

Dry ice is carbon dioxide, which is heavier than oxygen. So, remove the oxygen from the food.

The storage bucket is placed in another giant bucket filled with dry ice, and the oxygen leaves the bucket due to its lighter weight. Then you can seal the lid to store the food for long durations.

Oxygen Absorbers

There is yet another technique that can remove oxygen from food and prevent insects' growth inside the containers: using oxygen absorbers. They are considered even more effective than the vacuum sealing method. Oxygen absorbers are small packets containing iron powder.

The packets are made of materials that absorb oxygen and moisture but do not allow the iron or other chemicals to leak out of the bags.

Therefore, they are considered safe for human health. These bags are most appropriate for places with more humidity and a greater chance of oxidation.

Smoking

Smoking is just another method of dehydration. Instead of drying food in an electric dehydrator or other heating appliance, the dehydration is carried out through smoking.

It is most suitable to dehydrate meat as it removes moisture from the meat grains and dries out all the microbes.

Direct fire smoking was the method of the past, and today it can be carried out at home using electric smokers.

Wood chips are burned to produce smoke, which infuses a strong flavor into the meat and gradually dehydrates it. Meat jerky is often prepared using the smoking method. Once smoked, the jerky can then be stored without refrigeration in a clean, dry, and calm place like other non-perishable food items. As dehydration takes many hours, 24–46 at a minimum, you must prepare to invest an adequate amount of time. This preservation technique cannot work for instant storage.

Salting

Salting foods has been with humans for a long time, which is why salt was a precious commodity in the ancient world. No salt means no food storage.

No food storage means no nautical travel. No nautical travel means no empire. Perhaps all of history hinges on something as simple as nutrition, but that's a conversation for another time.

If you have access to lots of salt, you can use it to preserve beef and fish for a decent amount of time without any refrigeration. Salt removes the water. Microorganisms and bacteria can't survive long without moisture, so your meat can become inhospitable to the things that make it go wrong.

Salt Curing and Brining

It is an old method to preserve meat because the salt creates an inhospitable environment for bacteria and microorganisms.

You can rub the mixture of sugar and salt on the pieces of fresh meat, pack it tightly into a crock and store it in a stable place and cool temperature.

Brining will start the salt curing, but you can use additional brine solution that should be changed regularly. Salt-curing requires you to soak the meat in water for a long time to remove the excess salt and bring it to an edible level.

Freeze-Drying

Freeze-drying is not the same as dehydrating. Freeze-drying removes about 98% of the water content, while dehydration removes 80%. This means freeze-dried food lasts longer. The process is different, too. Freeze-dried food is frozen below zero in a vacuum chamber. The temperature is slowly raised, so the moisture in the food moves from a frozen form to a vapor, leaving the food. In the past, you couldn't freeze-dry at home. Now, Harvest Right sells an at-home freeze dryer. They are not cheap. A small one will cost you upwards of $2,100. It's an investment, but commercial freeze-dried food is also expensive. Freeze-drying all your food will likely cost less than buying the same amount from a company.

Freeze-dried meat will have the most extended shelf life of any meat in your stockpile. Sealed in its package, it can last up to 25 years. Once opened, you should eat it within the next few weeks.

Cellars for Roots

Root cellars are another age-old technique of preserving food if you have room for one. A root cellar, essentially a hole in the earth, maintains a consistent temperature and humidity throughout the year, offering a reasonably stable environment to keep food. While root cellars were initially used to keep potatoes and turnips, they may now be used to preserve almost any fruit or vegetable, with the probable exception of apples. These produce ethylene gas, which accelerates the ripening of other fruits.

A metal garbage can with a lid is a simple method to build a tiny root cellar. You want it close to your home, so you don't have to travel far to get there. Avoid placing it in a low-yard area where water will pool in a heavy storm. Dig a hole deep enough to bury the can, exposing the final few inches on a slight rise in the land. Put your treats in the can, then close the top. Toss several inches of hay over the lid, then cover it with a tarp to keep the rain off. Weigh down the tarp's edges to keep it from blowing away. Look at what you're leaving for later use every time you pull vegetables from the root cellar. Anything that is starting to decay or mold should be removed. Toss everything into the compost pile.

Immersion in Alcohol

In the same way, as salt and sugar do, alcohol pulls water from food, preventing the development of microbes. The ability to fully immerse tiny quantities of food in your preferred hard liquor will allow you to preserve them almost forever. Don't attempt to preserve excessive food in an insufficient amount of alcohol. Maximum water absorption is an important concept to understand. This food preservation technique is the most effective for producing flavor extracts and keeping foods with high acidities, such as fruit.

Preserving in Oil or Fat

The practice of smothering food with oil to keep out the air and avoid mold is centuries old. Oil, on the other hand, will keep bacteria that are present in food from spreading. Anaerobic bacteria (which do not need oxygen to survive), like Clostridium botulinum, may be harmful if they spread into an environment. Once dangerous germs have been eliminated, use rendered fat or oil to seal the food and preserve it. It is necessary to salt cure the meat before slowly cooking it and then covering it with fat to make animal products such as duck confit. Simmer them for 10 minutes in full-strength vinegar for veggies to bring out their natural sweetness. Pour out the vinegar and drizzle a high-quality oil like extra-virgin olive oil over the prepared meal to finish it. Add some zucchini, eggplant, and mushrooms to create an Italian-style antipasto.

Conclusion

No one likes to sit around and think about disaster scenarios and horrifying what-if situations. Still, it isn't wise to completely ignore the possibilities of a natural disaster, the act of war or economic collapse. Anything can happen. While we hope for the best, we must prepare for the worst.

If nothing ever happens, it isn't like the food will go to waste. It can be used as a supplement to your regular pantry if you replace what you use. Think of it as the stocked shelves in your local supermarket. Because you need to keep your food supply fresh, you will want to pull out stuff that is getting old and use it in your kitchen and replace the old stuff with new stock.

The skills you learn, such as dehydrating and canning food, are invaluable. There is no doubt food prices will continue to rise. You can save your family a ton of money by making home preservation a habit. You will be proud to feed the family food you have packaged with love and without many nasty chemicals and other potentially harmful preservatives.

You will also be handing down skills to your children, who will see the benefits of having emergency food storage and practice it in their own homes with their families. These are skills you want to pass down to your children. Lessons will help them live that long life we all envision for our children.

Today is the day you start planning for your future. You don't have to do it all at once, but you do need to take that first step. Come up with a strategy and start planning to begin your emergency food storage the next time you go to the market. Little by little, your storage will be built up, and you will feel better about it. Get your family involved, and your job will be that much easier.

Printed in Great Britain
by Amazon

45222148R00056